SINGLE YESTERDAY AND STILL SINGLE TODAY

60 Days of Encouraging Devotions for the Single Woman Desiring Marriage

Taliah Aneesah

CONTENTS

INTRODUCTION

T here is a significant number of devotionals available in the Christian space. Many deal with waiting
and trusting God's timing. Many devotionals are
geared towards topics specifically related to women, men,
or marriage. While there are devotionals geared toward
single women, there are just not enough. In the Christian
space, single people are overlooked. There is an an array
of options of Christian material related to marriage. There
are many resources available to encourage couples having
difficulties in their marriage. However, we cannot continue to overlook the single people who need encouragement.

While single men need just as much encouragement as
women, I write this devotional from my perspective as a
single woman. I chose to write this devotional specifically
for women. Christianity and society place a tremendous
amount of pressure on women to be married. Often individuals ask "what's wrong with her" anytime a woman is
not married. Many women desire to be married but choose
to wait on God to bring them marriage. It can be very
discouraging for a woman to continue year after year to remain single. This devotional is written to help encourage
single women who find themselves saying *Single Yesterday
and Still Single Today*. I hope that this devotional will en-

able you to keep trusting in God and waiting on Him to bring you your husband.

Day 1

THERE IS NOTHING WRONG WITH YOU

There is a time for everything, and a season for every activity

under the heavens.

Ecclesiastes 3:1 NIV

A m I too nice? Is it my personality? Is it something about my clothes or maybe my body? I know some of these thoughts have crossed your mind. Quite frankly these thoughts have probably crossed your mind on several occasions. When you've been single for so long, your mind tells you that you are the problem. Thoughts that there is something wrong with you can try to fill your mind. You think that you must be the reason why you are still single. You must be defective. Let me tell you a little secret. There is nothing wrong with you!

God has designed you and made you just the way He wanted to make you. It's time you stop thinking something is wrong with you and remember what the verse says: There is a time and season for everything. You are not married yet because it isn't God's appointed time for you to get married. God knows your desire for marriage and won't let you down. Although you want to be married right now, God has other plans. God will decide when the time is right for you to get married. God's timing is so much better than our own. Just think about how many times you wanted to do something right then and there, but God kept you from doing it. As you look back now, you thank God that He delayed you. The things we obtain by waiting on God's timing is always better than if we would have obtained them in our own timing. God will bring you your husband at the appointed time and season. As you wait on God continue to trust in His timing and not your own.

> *Lord, thank you for preparing a time and season for everything. Help me to wait on your timing. Assist me with trusting in your timing and not my own. Give me the confidence to know that there is nothing wrong with me. Even when I'm discouraged, allow me to remember you have a time and season for everything. Amen.*

Day 2

STOP TRYING TO CONTROL GOD'S TIMING

But God's not finished. He's waiting around to be gracious to you. He's gathering strength to show mercy to you. God takes the time to do everything right – everything. Those who wait around for him are the lucky ones.

Isaiah 30:18 MSG

As a single woman, I know you're accustomed to making things happen. Since you don't have a husband by your side, you control whether things get done or not. When you desire a certain meal for dinner, you cook it. If you want to go to a certain place you go. If you want to spend your day relaxing and reading a good book, you have the power to determine how you spend your day. You don't have to wait on anyone to do anything because you do it for yourself. This is what makes being a single woman great.

You can try to control many aspects of your life; however, there is one aspect of your life you can't control. You can't control when God decides to bring you into marriage. You can't speed up getting married or slow it down. No matter what you do or how hard you try, you simply can't control God's timing. God's timing is perfect. You desire to have marriage right now, but God is taking his time to do everything right. God is taking his time to mold you as a woman and to mold your husband. Be patient and wait on God to bring you marriage. He will give you the strength you need to wait as long as needed. Waiting for God's perfect timing may not be pretty, but it will be worth it. God will bring you the perfect husband for you and you alone. As the verse says, those who wait around for Him are the lucky ones. No matter how long it takes. Keep waiting on God. Trust his timeframe and know He will give you all the strength you need to keep waiting.

Father, forgive me when I try to control things that are outside of my control. Help me to wait on you and trust in your perfect timing. Give me the strength to keep waiting. Let me remember that you are not finished with me. Give me the faith to keep trusting in you and your word. Amen.

Day 3

GOD IS NEVER LATE

God isn't late with his promise as some measure lateness. He is restraining himself on account of you, holding back the End because he doesn't want anyone lost. He's giving everyone space and time to change.

2 Peter 3:9 MSG

Y ou picked up this devotional because the title spoke to you, *Single Yesterday and Still Single* today. You've asked the question "God, how long must I wait?" You've posed this question to God many times during your prayer time. In fact, you've asked this question many times while crying out to Him. It feels like life is passing you by. It feels like your best years are now behind you. You consistently pray for marriage but continue to remain single. You sense that God has forgotten about you. Do not fear though because God has not forgotten about you and God is never late. He will bring you into marriage when He sees fit.

God already has a set time for you. God may not be bringing you marriage because there is still work left to do on you. There are things about you that He still wants to change. He is giving you the space and time to change those things. God loves you enough to give you time to change those things now before those things wreak havoc in your future marriage. God has promised He will give you the desires of your heart. As long as it is in His will, He will bring you marriage. He isn't late with marriage. He is using this time to prepare you. Use this time to determine how you can become a better woman. Continue to trust in God's timing. He is waiting until the perfect time to bring you His promise.

God, thank you for loving me enough to withhold marriage until you have made me into the woman you want me to be. I ask that you give me more patience to trust in you and wait on your timing. Help me always remember that you are never late but always on time. Amen.

Day 4

SURRENDER GETTING MARRIED OVER TO GOD

Ask in my name, according to my will, and he'll most certainly

give it to you. Your joy will be a river overflowing its banks!

John 16:24 MSG

We know the Bible is filled with numerous verses in which God tells you to ask Him for what you want, and He will give it to you. We know God is faithful and if you ask Him for it, He will do it. It's important to remember as you ask God for things to make sure you are asking for them according to His will and in His name. There are so many things that we want but they aren't always in line with God's will for our lives. Just as you ask for other things, when you ask God for marriage you have to make sure it is what God has planned for your life.

If you truly desire to marry the man God has for you, then surrender getting married over to God. Let God guide you on your quest for marriage. Let Him bring you your husband. If you truly surrender it, you don't have to search for your husband. God already knows who your husband is even if you don't know right now. Surrendering over your marriage frees you from the anxiety and worry over the whens, hows, whos, and wheres of marriage. You don't have to try to figure anything out because He already has it figured out. There is no one who is more capable of bringing you the husband He has for you in His perfect timing then God, the Father, the Son, and the Holy Spirit. Focus on building and growing your relationship with God. Surrender getting married over to the Lord. Let Him handle that part while you do your part by growing closer in your relationship with the Lord.

Lord, I come to you today asking for you to free me of my worry and my anxiety surrounding marriage. Let me surrender whether I get married completely over to you. I don't want to keep trying to make marriage happen on my timetable or how I want it to happen. I surrender it all to you Father. In Jesus name I pray. Amen.

Day 5

KNOW WHO YOU ARE BEFORE MARRIAGE

"Haven't you read," he replied, "that at the beginning the Creator made them male and female, and said, 'For this reason a man will leave his father and mother and be united to his wife, and the two will become one flesh.'? So, they are no longer two, but one flesh. Therefore what God has joined together, let man not separate.

Matthew 19:4-6 NIV

Marriage is going to transform you. It will transform you in ways you never knew possible. Marriage, while wonderful and enjoyable, is still very hard work. As a wife you will become one with your husband. You will be forming a team with you, your husband and God. God doesn't want it to be two separate people making decisions about their marriage. God wants it to be a husband and wife working as a team. You will no longer be two but one. Although you will become one, you and your husband will still have your own identities. You will be a team of two identities coming together. It's important to know who you are before you get married. It's important to have your own identity.

As women, we are by nature nurturing and generally looking out for the needs of others. It can become so easy to define your identity based on what you can do for other people. Singleness is a good time to take a look in the mirror and really discover who you are as a woman. It's a time to understand your wants and needs. It's a time to establish your own hobbies and taste. Having your own identity before you become one with your husband will only enrich your marriage. Not only should you know who you are as a woman, but you should know who you are in Christ. Build a personal relationship with God before you ever marry. Get to know your identity in Christ. When the time is right, God will bring you and your husband together. You will no longer be two people, but one.

Lord, help me to learn who I am as a woman. Help me to learn who I am in you. Allow me to have a personal intimate relationship with you before I ever marry. Prepare me for who you will have me to be as a woman, as a wife, as a mother and as your daughter. In Jesus name. Amen.

Day 6

KEEP LIVING WHILE
WAITING ON MARRIAGE

Why am I so depressed? Why this turmoil within me? Put your hope

in God, for I will still praise Him, my Savior and my God.

Psalm 42:11 HCSB

That's it you've had enough. You're sick and tired of people telling you to keep trusting God. You're tired of people telling you "this too shall pass". You've heard it all and don't want to hear another encouraging or positive word. You've heard these things said so many times that the words don't encourage you anymore. You know as a Christian you're expected to keep trusting God. At this point you don't know if you can keep trusting in what you don't see. You're constantly battling with trusting God and not trusting Him. You've trusted God so much that you put certain things on hold because you were certain He was bringing you your husband soon. The soon you imagined is not the soon God had in His plans for you. In this single season, it's vital you keep living while waiting on marriage.

As women we may put off buying a house, switching careers, moving to that new city or other major life decisions because we're waiting for God to bring us our husband. Ideally you and your husband would be sharing those life experiences together. You have your plans but

God has other plans. His plans are for you to be single right now. God never intended for you to stop living while you wait on your husband. Don't put your dreams and goals on hold waiting on God to bring you marriage. God placed those in you for a reason. He will give you everything you need to accomplish them whether single or married. Don't put your life on hold. Keep working toward those goals and desires that God has placed in your heart. When God says it's time, He will bring your husband to you. Don't stop living in the meantime.

> *Lord, help me to continue to live while I wait on you. Don't let me fall victim to putting my goals and dreams on hold waiting to accomplish them with my husband. I know that you know what's best for me. If you want us to accomplish them together, you will let me know so. Give me the courage to continue to let your will be done in my life. Amen.*

Day 7

USE YOUR TIME OF SINGLENESS WISELY

I want you to live as free of complications as possible. When you're unmarried, you're free to concentrate on simply pleasing the Master. Marriage involves you in all the nuts and bolts of domestic life and in wanting to please your spouse, leading to so many more demands on your attention. The time and energy that married people spend on caring for and nurturing each other, the unmarried can spend in becoming whole and holy instruments of God. I'm trying to be helpful and make it as easy as possible for you, not make things harder. All I want is for you to be able to develop a way of life in which you can spend plenty of time together with the Master without a lot of distractions.

1 Corinthians 7:32-35 MSG

It's difficult to look at being single as a gift. It's extremely hard to look at it this way when you've been single for so long. You can't see how your singleness is a gift. Your tears and your loneliness don't seem to correspond with singleness being a gift. Yet God's word confirms that singleness is a gift. It is a time in your life where all you have to do is focus solely on God. You don't have to worry about trying to please and take care of your husband. You don't have to worry about sharing your time and your attention. At this point all you have to do is worry about spending time with the Lord.

You will never have this time of singleness again. It's time you look at it differently and start using it wisely. Use this time to fast and pray. Use this time to be still and hear from the Holy Spirit. Use this time to develop an intimate relationship with God. It is a lot easier to seek God right now than when you're being pulled in every direction by the demands of being a wife and mother. Don't spend these nights upset about being single. Spend these nights seeking God. Ask God what He wants to do and how He wants to use you while single. Now is the time to spend your days reading your word and praying to God. There will come a time when you will have to devote some of that time to your husband. During this time of singleness, you can devote all your time to your first love, God. Take this time to grow closer to God. Use your time of singleness wisely.

Lord, thank you for giving me this time of singleness. Help me to change my perspective and see it as the gift it is. Let me use my time to grow closer to you. Let me use this time to develop an intimate relationship with you. Help me to not be blinded by distractions and my emotions. Allow me to devote all my time to you. In Jesus name. Amen.

Day 8

GOD IS BUILDING
YOUR FAITH

So let's do it-full of belief, confident that we're presentable

inside and out. Let's keep a firm grip on the promises

that keep us going. He always keeps his word.

Hebrews 10:22-23 MSG

Your single season has purpose. You haven't been waiting this long for no reason. God is using this time to build your faith in Him. God has already given you His promises. He is using this time to strengthen your faith. Learn to have a faith that is able to move mountains. All it takes is to have faith the size of a mustard seed.

Go through this single season full of belief and confidence. Don't lose sight of the promises God has given you. Allow this time to be one in which your faith is strengthened. God is preparing you for marriage because marriage won't always be easy. There will be times when all you have to stand on is your faith in God. There will be times when your faith is what keeps you going. God is building your faith for marriage but also for life. When you go through trials and tribulations, your faith in God is what will help you through. Your faith must be strong enough to carry your husband when he struggles with his faith. Our Heavenly Father knows what He is doing in your season of singleness. Don't be discouraged because marriage is taking so long to come. Trust in God's process and let Him build your faith as you wait on Him.

Lord, at times I don't understand why you continue to keep me single. I know you have a plan for my life, and you know what you're doing. Let me be encouraged in this season. Build my faith in you. Let me have faith that can move mountains. Keep me strong in you, Lord. Amen.

Day 9

GET YOUR SPIRITUAL
LIFE IN ORDER FIRST

But seek first the kingdom of God and His righteousness,

and all these things will be provided for you.

Matthew 6:33 HCSB

A s a wife, one of your duties will be to help to nurture your family. You'll always be there for your husband and for your kids. This will be no small task. It's important you equip yourself with the tools needed to accomplish this task. More than anything the most important tool you need will be God. Before you hone your skills in cooking, child rearing, being supportive to your husband or any other wifely duties, get your spiritual life in order first.

You won't be able to handle the demands of being a wife if your relationship with God is slacking. Seek God before you seek anything else. Learn who He is before you ever learn how to be a wife. God wants to show you how to love by loving you. You need to have a relationship with God to learn how to love and be a wife. Seek God as you pray for your husband. Surrender marriage to him. Search Him to know His will for your marriage. God hears your prayers and will send your husband to you when He sees fit. Don't focus on how to be a wife before you focus on how to be a Christian woman. You will always be a child of God before you are a wife or mother. Prioritize your relationship with God. Get your spiritual life in order and watch God work.

Father, I want to know you on a deeper level. Lead me closer to you and your will for my life. Help me to seek you and your righteousness before I become a wife. Teach me how to love you before I ever love anyone else. Amen.

Day 10

IT'S NOT UP TO YOU TO FIND YOUR HUSBAND

A man who finds a wife finds a good thing and obtains favor from the Lord.

Proverbs 18:22 HCSB

Have you ever met a guy that you felt like was everything you wanted in a husband? Did you get excited thinking you had finally found your husband? Now be honest, did you also find yourself pursuing that man or even chasing after him? Sometimes when we see something we want we go after it. Occasionally we can forget that God's word says a man who finds a wife finds a good thing. It is the man who finds the wife not the other way around. It's not up to you to find your husband.

God has your husband picked out for you. He will place you in the right place for your husband to find you. You don't have to go searching for him. He is in the process of searching for you. Your job is to seek God and prepare to be found. Make sure that you'll be ready to be the wife God has designed you to be. Focus on being ready as a woman to be found by your husband. Until that time focus on God and develop into who He has designed you to be. At the appointed time, your husband will find his good thing in you as his wife.

Father, forgive me for those times I have tried to find my husband instead of trusting that you will allow him to find me. Let me continue to seek you and work on becoming the woman and the wife you have designed me to be. I ask that you give me the knowledge, wisdom and the tools to become that person. Amen.

Day 11

ENJOY YOUR SINGLENESS

I don't think the way you think. The way you work isn't the way I work.

God's Decree. For as the sky soars high above earth, so the way I work sur-

passes the way you work, and the way I think is beyond the way you think.

Isaiah 55:8-9 MSG

D o you ever sit and ask God what's His plan? You want to know exactly what He's doing. Do you wonder why is it that year after year you continue to be single? I know at times, correction, a lot of times you just don't understand why you're still single. If it was up to you, you would have already married some time ago. You aren't choosing to continue to be single, but it's what God is choosing for you right now. He is working on your behalf. Whether you can see it or not, know that God is working.

God has chosen at this moment in time to allow you to remain single. No, you might not understand it because God doesn't always work the way we think or want Him to work. Don't become frustrated, you have a gift right now. That gift is singleness. Enjoy this gift while you have it. You will never get back this time. You will never be able to do what you want to do, when you want to do it and not have to answer to anyone. You won't be able to keep your house either as clean or as unclean as you want without affecting someone else. You won't be able to sit with that acne medicine splattered across your face without anyone seeing it. Even though you desire a husband and oftentimes feel lonely, take this time and enjoy it. You don't want to look back at your time of singleness and realize you spent the whole time anxious and worried about when you would get married. God works and thinks in ways that are beyond us. God will bring you your husband in time. Until that time enjoy the gift of singleness you have before you.

Father, help me to remember that your ways are not my ways and your thoughts are not my thoughts. Open my eyes to see the gift of singleness that you have in front of me. Let me not waste this time but enjoy this time. Give me the strength to keep waiting and trusting you. Amen.

Day 12

LIVE AS SOMEONE YOU WOULD WANT TO MARRY

It's in Christ that we find out who we are and what we are living for. Long before we first heard of Christ and got our hopes up, he had his eye on us, had designs on us for glorious living, part of the overall purpose he is working out in everything and everyone.
Ephesians 1:11-12 MSG

It's important for you to know who you are as a woman before you ever meet your husband. Know who you are as a woman, but more importantly know who you are in Christ. Find out what He has called you to do and who He has called you to be. Take this time now to develop into that person. You don't want to meet your husband and not be ready for Him because you're still trying to figure out who you are. Let God lead you and show you how to become the wife, mother and woman He wants you to be. Become that person now. Become someone you would want to marry.

It's important to focus on knowing who you are while single. While your husband is preparing for marriage, make sure you use your time to become a person you would want to marry. Use this single season to work on yourself. Don't expect the other person to be the only one doing the work. Learn what God's design is for marriage and for wives. Study His word and practice it. Become the wife you are called to be so that when God says it's time you'll be ready to embark on marriage.

> *God, I ask that you continue to work on me in my season of singleness. Make me into the wife, mother, and woman you have called me to be. Help me to learn who I am in you and who you have called me to be. Guide me as I work to become all that you want me to be. In Jesus name. Amen.*

Day 13

DESIRE A CHRISTIAN MARRIAGE, NOT JUST A MARRIAGE

I am the vine; you are the branches. The one who remains in Me and I in

him produces much fruit, because you can do nothing without Me.

John 15:5 HCSB

The fact that you're reading this devotional is evidence that you desire to be married. If you didn't desire marriage, you wouldn't have picked up this book. It's easy to get wrapped up in the idea of getting married: daydreaming and counting the days until you're happily married with the husband God has for you. Desiring marriage is great. Make sure that you don't just desire a marriage but desire a Christian marriage.

Just as the verse says you can do nothing without God. Marriage is something that's hard and takes a lot of work. If you go into a marriage without God, your marriage will be even tougher. Let God be at the center of your marriage. Desire to have a marriage that is filled with Him. When times get hard, you will need to lean on the Lord to help you in your marriage. Make sure that your desires are in check. Make sure that you aren't praying and asking for just a marriage. Pray and ask God for a Christian marriage. Remain in God no matter what. Even though this single season is difficult, continue to seek God. He will not just bring you any old marriage, but God will bring you the Christian marriage He has for you as long as you remain in Him. Trust God and keep seeking Him.

Lord, help me to remain in you. I know that I can do nothing without you. Father I ask that you not only bring me into marriage but let my marriage be one filled with you. Lord be at the center of my future marriage. Help me to grow closer to you and help the husband you have for me to grow closer to you. Let us remain in you no matter what circumstances we face in our life. Amen.

Day 14

STOP COMPARING YOURSELF TO OTHER WOMEN

However, as it is written: What no eye has seen, what no
ear has heard, and what no human mind has conceived the
things God has prepared for those who love him.
1 Corinthians 2:9 NIV

It's quite easy to find yourself scrolling on social media for an hour. You planned on only being on there for ten minutes. Ten minutes turned into a full hour. Before you logged on to social media you felt fine. Now after you've logged off you feel a little down. Now you're feeling sad about being single. You spent a whole hour comparing yourself to every woman's timeline you ran across. There is no need to compare yourself to any other woman. God's word says no one has seen, heard or conceived what He has prepared for you.

What God has for you is for you. God loves you and has prepared so many wonderful things just for you. God has prepared a special husband just for you. You don't have to compare yourself to other women. Don't feel like you need to change who you are or be more like them. God has designed you exactly the way He wants you to be, and no one can take away what He has for you. No other woman will have the husband God has for you. Don't keep comparing yourself to your friends, your family, or women you see on social media. You don't have to become more like them to get what they have. Seek God and wait for Him to bring you the things He has for you. God loves you.

Father, free me from comparison. Help me to be confident in who you have made me to be. Let me trust you and continue to wait on you to bring me the things you have prepared for me. In Jesus name. Amen.

Day 15

EVERY GUY YOU MEET ISN'T YOUR HUSBAND

Search and read the scroll of the Lord: Not one of them will be

missing, none will be lacking its mate, because He has ordered

it by my mouth, and He will gather them by His Spirit.

Isaiah 34:16 HCSB

I know when you read this verse you get really excited. It says that God won't forget about you. You won't be lacking your mate. This verse is telling you the Lord is going to bring you your husband. You are encouraged by reading the Bible but also frustrated by what it says God will do for you. The problem is you don't know when God is going to fulfill His word. You don't know when you're going to get married. You try not to get overly excited every time you meet a new guy. You contemplate whether this guy might just be your mate. Continue to have faith because God's word tells you, you won't be lacking your mate. This means God will bring you marriage if it is His will for your life.

At times we can be blinded by this verse and others. We can overlook the red flags from a man because we think this one may be "The One." Every guy that shows you attention isn't worthy of your attention. Yes, God is going to bring you your husband. God will do it according to His will. Don't keep stressing and worrying about whether or not the guy you meet is the husband God has for you. Take time to listen to the Holy Spirit. Let the Holy Spirit guide you and reveal your husband to you. It's hard to relax and stop stressing over if the next guy or maybe the next guy may just be your husband. Take time to focus on God. His word is true. It tells us we will not be lacking a mate. Stay in God's will and He will bring you marriage according to His perfect plan.

Lord, let your will be done and not my will. Free me from worry and anxiety about which man is my husband. Let me turn to you and seek the Holy Spirit's guidance. I ask that you give me clarity when you're ready to reveal to me my husband. Until then let me continue to focus on you. In Jesus name I pray. Amen.

Day 16

IT'S JUST NOT TIME YET

Don't panic. I'm with you. There's no need to fear for I'm your God. I'll give you strength. I'll help you. I'll hold you steady, keep a firm grip on you.
Isaiah 41 : 10 MSG

It seems like the years continue to tick by and yet you remain single. You have a desire to be married by a certain age. As you continue to get closer to that age or maybe the age has even passed, it's difficult to not panic. You probably thought you'd already be married for years by now. Maybe you imagined by now the two of you would have traveled to various countries. The two of you would have shared many experiences by now. In fact, maybe you thought right now you would have a child or at least be pregnant. As much as you had things planned out, none of it has happened yet. Don't become fearful and try to make things happen on your own.

Yes, you will be discouraged at times. You'll try to figure out what is wrong with you as a woman. You'll try to figure out what you can do to speed the process along. The thought will cross your mind to change who you are because you start thinking that who you are is the problem. No not at all! There is nothing wrong with you! Don't panic and become fearful. Don't start changing who you are to get a husband. God has made you exactly the way He wanted you to be. Accept the fact that it's just not time yet. Leave it all in the Lord's hands. The Bible tells us He is with us. God is going to give you the ability to continue to wait for Him to bring your husband to you. Be encouraged today knowing God has you in His firm grip. He will keep you steady and help you through this season. When it's time, God will bring you your husband.

Father, I come to you today asking for your strength. I ask that you hold me steady as I continue through this waiting season. Free me from the fear that you won't bring me my husband. Help me be confident in my waiting season knowing you are with me and will help me. Amen.

Day 17

AM I BEING PUNISHED FOR PAST SINS

And we know that God causes all things to work together for good to those who love God, to those who are called according to His purpose.

Romans 8:28 NASB

You've spent a lot of time praying and seeking God. You've spent time preparing yourself for marriage. You feel like you're doing your part but with each day that passes you continue to be single. You start to reflect on your past and some of the decisions you made. While you are trusting God now that wasn't always the case. In your past you lived more for yourself than for God. There are some decisions in your past that you're not proud of today. You wonder if maybe those decisions, maybe those past sins are the reasons why you're still single. You ask yourself "Am I being punished for my past sins?"

The answer to this question is NO. God is not punishing you for your past sins. That is not the way God works. God offers you grace, mercy and forgiveness for your past decisions and your past sins. He doesn't condemn you or punish you for your past. God loves you and gives you new grace every day. Just as the verse says God causes all things to work together for good. God has a purpose for your life. He isn't delaying you from marriage to punish you but to help you. God is preparing you for everything He has for you. He won't bring you marriage until He knows His daughter is ready. Don't regret or feel disappointment about your past any longer. God has already forgiven you. He knows exactly what He's doing. He will bring you into marriage when He sees fit. Just trust Him. He causes all things to work together for good. You love God, now let God love you.

Lord, thank you for your grace and your mercy. Thank you for forgiving me of my sins. I ask that you break me free from my past. Help me to stop regretting my past or being disappointed by it. Father help me to remember that you love me and forgive me even when I don't forgive myself. Thank you for loving me and never giving up on me. In Jesus name. Amen.

Day 18

YOUR TEARS WON'T
ALWAYS BE THERE

Do not let your hearts be troubled. You believe in God; believe also in me.

John 14:1 NIV

Y ou are at a point where you really want to give up on marriage. You're so tired of being alone and lonely. Yes, you know that just because you are alone doesn't mean you have to be lonely. You've heard that before. You believe it's true. However, let's be honest, you're still human. You're a woman who desires to be married one day. While maybe not all the time, some days you feel lonely. Some days you feel alone. Some days all you can do is cry when you think about just how single you really are. You cry when you think about how much you desire marriage, but marriage continues to escape you. It's okay to cry.

Keep crying even though no one knows you're crying. You put on a brave face in public but some nights all you do is cry. It's okay to cry, there is nothing wrong with crying. Realize your tears won't always be there. Your heart won't always be troubled. God is there for you if you just keep trusting Him. He sees your tears and hears your cries. He knows when you feel lonely and when you feel alone. Trust in your Father and trust in Jesus. God sent Jesus to save you and to be there when you have no one else. Keep being faithful and keep believing. God won't leave your heart distressed. In his perfect timing, He will bring you marriage. Cry your tears but find comfort in knowing your tears won't always be there.

Lord Jesus, hear my prayers. Father, sometimes all I can do is cry. Some days all I can do is shed tears even when I don't want to shed them. Wipe my tears away Lord. Help me to keep trusting you even when I can't see you through my tears. I trust you. I know that you hear my prayers and you see my tears. I know one day you will wipe my tears away. Thank you, Jesus for hearing my prayer. Amen.

Day 19

GOD IS USING YOUR EXPERIENCE TO HELP OTHERS

You did not choose me, but I chose you and appointed you so that you might go and bear fruit—fruit that will last—and so that whatever you ask in my name the Father will give you. This is my command: Love each other.

John 15:16-17 NIV

Another year has passed and you're still single. You don't understand why God is delaying you. You don't understand why this season of singleness has lasted so long. You were on board initially with God's plans. You were on board when you thought you'd only be single for just a few more months or just one more year. Yet you look up and years have passed and you're still single. It is challenging to not get frustrated and angry with God. You want to be married and you just don't understand why God hasn't brought you marriage. You may continue to be single for this long because God is using your single experience to help others. God wants you to use your experience with singleness to go bear fruit.

God will bring you marriage when He sees fit. Your single season may be lasting this long because He wants to use you to help others. The Lord wants you to remember your tears, your frustration, and your anguish. Use that to encourage other single people. You know firsthand what it feels like to desire marriage but continue to be single. You continue to be strong and have faith in Him no matter how long it is taking. Perhaps one of your friends, church members or co-workers may be struggling with being single. You may be the only person someone can turn to who would understand what they are going through. You understand how they feel and can relate to the loneliness they are going through. God wants you to be an example to those around you. He wants you to help others stay faithful even when they are feeling alone and lonely. Don't look at this single season as just a long waiting period. Use your single season to help others stay encouraged during their own single season.

Father, help me to not get frustrated with how long my single season is lasting. Let me use this experience to encourage others in their single season and in anything they are waiting on. Thank you for showing me how to have patience. Use me Lord to bear fruit as I wait on you. In Jesus name. Amen.

Day 20

CHANGE FROM THE INSIDE OUT

So here's what I want you to do, God helping you: Take your everyday, ordinary life your sleeping, eating, going to work, and walking around life and place it before God as an offering. Embracing what God does for you is the best thing you can do for him. Don't become so well-adjusted to your culture that you fit into it without even thinking. Instead, fix your attention on God. You'll be changed from the inside out. Readily recognize what he wants from you, and quickly respond to it. Unlike the culture around you, always dragging you down to its level of immaturity, God brings the best out of you, develops well-formed maturity in you.

Romans 12:1-2 MSG

C an you think back to a year ago or perhaps even five years ago? Think about how much God has changed you since that time. Think about how your relationship with God has grown since that time. Even though you're ready to throw in the towel and give up on ever being married, don't give up. God is working on you. He is changing you from the inside out. Look at how much He has already done! God wants you to continue to surrender your life to Him so He can continue to do His work on you.

God wants you to give Him all of your life not just parts of it. He wants the good and the bad parts. He wants you to place all your attention on Him and stop worrying about when you'll get married. He wants to change you from the inside out. Don't keep looking on social media and getting upset because you don't have what others have. Don't look at your friends and family and get sad because you don't have what they have. God won't bring you what they have because He will bring you what He has for you. God asks you to surrender every area of your life to Him including marriage. He wants you to seek Him and not seek the approval of others. Don't try to change to please other people thinking this will bring you marriage. You don't have to change yourself because God is changing you. Just let Him handle it. God will continue to change you from the inside out. When He sees you're ready, He will bring you your husband. Let go of control and let God work.

Father, allow me to let go of control. Help me to stop trying to change myself and let you change me. I thank you for everything you've already done for me. Don't let me be influenced or discouraged by what I see on social media and from those around me. Let my eyes stay lifted toward you. Lord I surrender my life to you. Amen.

Day 21

STUDY THE WORD

How can a young person live a clean life? By carefully reading the map of your Word. I'm single-minded in pursuit of you; don't let me miss the road signs you've posted.

Psalms 119:9-10 MSG

Take some time to think back to being in school. When it came time for you to take a test, did you take that test without studying for it? Well, some of you might have, but most of us never took a test without studying for it first. We took time to practice the homework and studied the textbook. We wanted to get a good grade on the test, so we took time to study the material. Approach life in a similar manner to how you approached that test in school. Life is not one test that we have to prepare for but years of many tests. In school it was the history or math textbook. This time the textbook is the Bible.

The Bible is filled with God's word. Your goal in life should be to live a life that is pleasing to God. The only way to do that is by studying God's word through reading and hearing it. God's word is the map for your life. If you want to gain strength to wait on God to bring your husband, study His word. There are scriptures to help you. If you want God to bring you into marriage study God's word to know what a Godly marriage looks like. Study the word to know how to fight the temptations you are faced with as a single woman. God's word will help you to live the life He wants you to live. He will use His word to give you guidance, wisdom, and knowledge in your single season. God wants to make you into the wife He has called you to be. In order to do that you must seek God and study His word.

Lord, I ask that you give me the discipline to study your word. I desire to study your word but sometimes I just don't seem to find the time to study your word. I ask that you shift my priorities around. I ask that you help me to make spending time with you and studying your word my first priority. In Jesus name. Amen.

Day 22

YOU'RE DOING IT HIS WAY BUT STILL SINGLE

For the Lord God is a sun and shield. The Lord gives grace and glory;

He does not withhold the good from those who live with integrity.

Psalms 84:11 HCSB

B y now you've been on this single journey for a while. God has revealed many things to you. He told you to change your habits, change your attitude, and change your surroundings. God led you to remove some of the people in your life and to stop going to certain places. He completely changed the way you date. God told you to do all these things and more. You're doing your best to listen and obey Him. You've changed so much. You have decided to trust God and start doing it His way. Yet you are still single.

It's very discouraging when you're doing your best to do things God's way and still remain single. It feels like all those changes you've made are in vain. You feel like you're the only one trying to truly do it God's way but everyone else is doing it their way and getting what you desire. Despite how you feel right now it won't always be this way. God loves you and wants His best for you. He sees your devotion and obedience to Him. God will give you grace and strength to keep waiting for Him. Don't be frustrated or discouraged because you're still single. God will not withhold the good from you if you live with integrity and according to His will. God will not withhold what He has for you if you continue to seek Him and trust Him. Keep doing it God's way. You won't be single forever.

God, forgive me for being impatient. Help me to trust you and remember that your way is best. Lord help me to keep growing into the woman that you want me to be. Give me the strength to keep going even when I want to give up on you. Order my steps, Father. Amen.

Day 23

DESIRES OF YOUR HEART

Delight yourself in the Lord, And He will give you the desires of your heart.

Psalm 37:4 NASB

The reason you're reading this devotional is because you have a desire to be married. If you didn't have this desire, you would've bypassed this book. It's important to keep that desire for marriage aligned with God's will. Sometimes we can lose sight of keeping our desires within God's will. Just because you desire marriage, it doesn't give you free rein to go marry the first man who seems promising. Desire for God to bring you marriage with the man He has picked out for you.

It's important during your single season to continue to chase after God. Don't let your desires blind you nor distract you. Let this season be a time where you delight yourself in the Lord. Seek God and spend this time with Him. Use this time to read your Bible every day. Use this time to spend it attending your local church. Use this time to serve and get involved in your church. Use this time to learn to serve others and put others first. You'll never get this time back so make sure you're taking advantage of it. God knows your deepest secrets and every single one of your desires. God is just waiting on you to give Him the control. Give your desires to God and He will give you the desires of your heart.

Father, I have a strong desire for marriage. I ask that you let my desire for marriage be healthy and not one of idolatry. I surrender control of it all over to you. Let me delight myself in you Lord. I ask that you let your will be done and not my will. In Jesus name. Amen.

Day 24

HE'S THERE

If your heart is broken, you'll find God right there, if you're

kicked in the gut, he'll help you catch your breath.

Psalm 34:18 MSG

Have you reached the point where you feel like giving up? Do you feel like God has answered everyone's prayers but yours? Have you tried and tried but nothing seems to work? It's alright to feel this way. It's difficult to continue to stay positive and optimistic when you don't see anything changing. It's tough to stay hopeful for marriage when you feel like you're not taking any steps forward. It's frustrating to keep trusting when you feel like God has left you all alone. Though you may feel alone, know that you're never alone. God is always there.

There may come a point in your life where you're tired of crying to your friends and family about being single. You keep dating but keep getting hurt. Maybe you want to date but never get asked out. These things leave you feeling defeated and utterly heartbroken. Though your heart is broken, He's there. Even when you feel like you have nothing left, He's there. Even when you feel lonely, He's there. When your friends and family have all disappeared, He's there. When you get frustrated and angry with God, He's still there. Although you feel like you're doing this thing on your own you're not. God is right there with you every step of the way. God is with you when your heart is broken. God is with you when you cry those tears. God is with you when you've lost all hope of ever being married. God has been, is and will always be there for you. Let your faith and hope for marriage be renewed because He's there.

Father, I cry out to you Lord because I need your help. I get discouraged and feel hopeless sometimes. I get angry and frustrated sometimes. Father give me strength to continue on. Help me to remember even when I feel all alone you are always there. Thank you for never leaving me. Amen.

Day 25

GOD WILL HELP YOU

I lift my eyes toward the mountains. Where will my help come from?

Psalm 121:1 HCSB

The Lord protects you; the Lord is a shelter right by your side.

Psalm 121:5 HCSB

You may feel a little helpless right now. This single season is lasting a lot longer than you ever imagined it would last. Another Christmas has passed and yet again you were the only one who showed up single. Another birthday has passed. You enjoy spending your birthday with friends and family but long to be able to spend it with just you and your husband. You keep trying to do everything right, but nothing seems to be changing. You don't know what else you can do. But therein lies the problem. You continue to try to do it all on your own. Instead of letting God do it, you keep trying to do it yourself.

God is the only one who can help you. There comes a point where you can't help yourself any longer. You've done everything you know to do in your own power. It's at this moment that you have to remember to look up. Look up and turn to God He will give you help. He will supply you with all the help you need. When you feel like giving up, God will be there to help you to keep going. He is there for you and is protecting you. God protects you even when you need to be protected from yourself. He is right there with you. He will never leave your side. When you feel helpless and all your hope of ever being married is gone, lift your eyes up. God will help you.

Father, I keep trying to do this thing on my own but I know I can't. I feel helpless right now. It feels like I'll always be single. I'm looking for you. I need your help Lord. Restore hope back to me. In Jesus name. Amen.

Day 26

NOT ONLY ARE YOU SINGLE BUT YOU'RE SUPER SINGLE

That's why I urge you to pray for absolutely everything,
ranging from small to large. Include everything as you embrace
this God-life, and you'll get God's everything.

Mark 11:24 MSG

There is being single and then there is being super single. Super single is when you aren't dating anyone. You aren't even talking or texting anyone on the phone. You literally are not being pursued by anyone. Being super single can be disheartening. It's easier to stay encouraged about marriage when you have a man taking you out on dates. It's easier when you have a man calling you on the phone. When none of those things are happening, it's hard to keep praying. You may feel a little guilty because you're not only praying for marriage but there are times when you're praying just to have a man to call you so you won't be super single.

Single in any form is extremely challenging when you've been waiting for a long time. It's tough when you have a strong desire for marriage. There are so many things you can do while you're single and waiting on God to bring you marriage. However, the most important thing to do is to keep seeking God. God's word tells you to pray about everything. No matter how trivial you think it is, pray about it. God is the one person you can talk to about anything. He won't judge you. Pray for God to move you from being super single to just maybe single and then marriage. It's okay. It may seem silly, but God already tells you to pray for everything. He won't ever judge you. God is the best listener. He will listen even when you think He can't hear you. Seek and pray to God about marriage. He will answer.

> *Lord, I come to you today because Lord I'm feeling lonely. I need you to give me the strength to keep praying. You know I'm super single and not dating or talking to anyone. Being super single makes my wait so much harder. I need your help to keep going despite what I see. Lift me up Father when I am weak. Amen.*

Day 27

YOU SMILE ON THE OUTSIDE BUT CRY ON THE INSIDE

It's what we trust in but don't yet see that keeps us going.

2 Corinthians 5:7 MSG

For we walk by faith, not by sight.

2 Corinthians 5:7 HCSB

How many times have you heard this verse? How many times has someone used this verse to encourage you as you struggle with being single? You know that you need to have faith in God. You're reading this devotional because you have faith in God. People around you see that smile on your face and hear your positive words. People hear you talk about remaining faithful even if you don't see how you're ever going to get married. People look at you and see how you don't let being single stop you from living your life. All of that is great and wonderful, but what people don't know is you smile on the outside but cry on the inside.

You put on a brave face for others but when you're alone there are nights when you cry all night long. There are days when that smile you have is hiding all your fears, anxieties and insecurities about being single. Don't feel alone in this because God sees what's behind your smile. God knows what you need and when you need it. Keep trusting God even though you don't see how marriage can ever happen for you. Have faith in the things you can't see. Let your faith and trust in God keep you going when you're running out of smiles. Let your faith and trust in God keep you going when you can't see what His next step is. He knows your desire for marriage. You can't see it but marriage is already in His plans for you. Have faith no matter what your situation looks like. God's got you.

Lord, I want to walk by faith and not by sight. But Lord the sight in front of me is so discouraging and cloudy. Turn my eyes to see past what I see and have faith in what I know I will see one day. Let my smile stop masking my pain and be one full of your joy and glory. Help me to remember all that you have done, are doing, and will do for me. I love you Father. Amen.

Day 28

GOD MAY NEED THIS TIME TO WORK ON YOUR HUSBAND

*Do not be mismatched with unbelievers. For what partnership
is there between righteousness and lawlessness? Or what
fellowship does light have with darkness?*
2 Corinthians 6:14 HCSB

You've spent many years being single. You've spent your nights alone. You've been to that place where all you can do is call on the name of Jesus because your loneliness is so overwhelming. You've been to that place where God is the only thing that keeps you going. Quite frankly, you've put in the work and you've put in your time. You feel like you're finally now the woman God wants you to be for marriage. You're ready for God to bring your husband and you together in marriage. This may all be true. However just because you're ready doesn't mean your husband is ready.

God's word tells us not to be matched with un-believers. Maybe you have remained single for this long because God needs this time to work on your husband. Perhaps your future husband may not be an unbeliever, but he may not have the relationship with God he needs to have. God has made the husband the leader of the house-hold. God wants to prepare your husband to be the leader of your household. The husband God has for you may not be in the place God wants him to be so that He can present him to you. God loves you and wants what is best for you. He wants to bring you a man who is seeking Him first. God's will is for your husband to love you as God loves the church. The man God has for you must spend time developing an intimate relationship with God so he will know how to love you. Be encouraged knowing that God is using this time to prepare your husband. God loves you so much that He wants to present to you His absolute best. Continue to wait on God as He prepares your husband. Don't try to rush things or get ahead of God's timing. Trust God because He knows best.

> *Father, lead and guide me on what you're doing in my season of singleness. Give me patience to wait on you and trust you. I know you're preparing your very best for me as you work on my husband. Let me let go of control and let you work on him. Help me to not grow weary as I wait. Show me when you have brought my husband to me. Amen.*

Day 29

IT'S TIME TO LET GO

Therefore, as God's chosen people, holy and dearly loved, clothe yourselves with compassion, kindness, humility, gentleness and patience. Bear with each other and forgive one another if any of you has a grievance against someone. Forgive as the Lord forgave you. And over all these virtues put on love, which binds them all together in perfect unity.

Colossians 3:12-14 NIV

It's time to let go of all the bitterness and hurt from your past. It's time to let go of the grudges you have with people. It's time to stop replaying those painful memories in your head. It's time to let go of that man who broke your heart. It's time to let go of that man that you really wanted to marry but the relationship didn't work out. It's time to let go of all of those things and start forgiving. Forgiveness will set you free from everything you have held on to. Think about everyone who has wronged you. Think about every unfair situation. Now let it go.

God wants you to use your season of singleness to let go. Let go of your past and forgive. God has, is, and will continue to forgive you. Stop expecting God to forgive you when you can't forgive others. Stop expecting Him to forgive you when you can't even forgive yourself. Forgive yourself for all your wrong choices. Forgive yourself for all those situations you wished you would have handled differently. Replace all that pain, hurt, and unforgiveness with compassion, kindness, humility, gentleness and patience. These are the traits that you need to be the wife and also the woman God has called you to be. Stop practicing unforgiveness and start practicing love. There will be plenty of times that you have to forgive your husband. Start practicing forgiveness now by letting all those things go. The time to start forgiveness is now.

Lord, break the chains of unforgiveness off my heart. Give me the strength to let go of my past hurts. Give me the strength to forgive all those who have wronged me. Heal my wounded heart. Replace the unforgiveness in my heart with love. Give me a pure heart. Amen.

Day 30

NEVER STOP GROWING

But grow in grace and knowledge of our Lord and Savior Jesus Christ. To him be glory both now and forever! Amen.

2 Peter 3:18 NIV

Have you spent years and years seeking God? Have you devoted a significant amount of time to reading your Bible? Do you feel like you have gone to every singles' and women's small group out there? You feel like you've spent so much time with God that you know him like the back of your hand. You feel like you know all there is about waiting on God to bring you your husband that you could even write a book. At times it can feel like you are starting to become stagnant with your relationship and knowledge of God. The key to overcoming this feeling is to never stop growing.

God has a limitless amount of grace and knowledge. Even when you feel like you've reached that desired place never stop desiring to go further. There is always something new to learn as, not only a woman, but also about God. Throughout marriage you'll need to be still and listen to hear from God. You need an intimate relationship with God to hear from Him. Continue to spend time seeking God and growing closer to Him every day. You will never reach a point where you can't grow in the knowledge and grace of God. When you want to grow, turn to God, He will take you to a new level. Use this season to grow and deepen your relationship with God.

> *Lord, at times I feel like my relationship with you has become stagnant. I ask that you never let our relationship become stagnant and always allow it to grow. Help me to grow in my knowledge of you and your grace. Guide me as I become the woman you have called me to be. Amen.*

Day 31

IT WON'T ALWAYS FEEL LIKE THIS

For His anger lasts only a moment, but His favor, a lifetime.

Weeping may spend the night, but there is joy in the morning.

Psalm 30:5 HCSB

This verse is a pretty common one. We normally hear it when someone is experiencing an unfavorable health diagnosis or have recently lost a loved one. Those situations bring forth a lot of weeping and a lot of pain. Many people may not realize it, but because you've been single for so long you also endure a lot of pain. A season of singleness can be filled with shedding tears over being lonely and discouraged. At some point the tears may dry up. You become so tired and weary that you have no more tears to cry. Don't lose hope and don't lose faith. Joy will come in the morning.

God will wash your tears away. Those feelings of discouragement, hopelessness, and sadness won't always be there. He will replace those feelings of loneliness with love from your husband. Yes, you love God with all your heart, but we know the love from a husband, who will be your companion and your best friend, is a different type of love. This love is great because it's the love God designed. One day God will wipe your frustration from singleness away. It won't always feel like this. Your joy is coming.

Lord, thank you that my joy is coming in the morning. I don't know which morning, Lord, but I am encouraged because I know one of these mornings my joy is coming. Help me to stay encouraged and not give up. Wash my tears away and renew my hope. In Jesus name. Amen.

Day 32

LET GOD BE YOUR NUMBER ONE

You're all I want in heaven! You're all I want on earth!

Psalm 73:25 MSG

One day you may wake up and realize God has moved down quite a few places on your list of priorities. It wasn't intentional; it just happened. Your career became more demanding and required more of your time. You were tired of sitting at home by yourself all the time, so you started spending more time with your friends. You didn't want to skip that Bible study or small group but you had two other organization's meetings at the same time. You didn't mean to press the snooze on your alarm and wake up late. Now you're running behind and don't have time to spend a few minutes with God. You didn't purposely shift your priorities but now you realize that if you're not more careful God will lose his number one spot.

Don't let your frustration with being single turn you into a woman too busy for God. Don't fill up your schedule with busyness and not have time for God. Let God be your number one. Don't ever neglect your relationship with God. If you don't have time for anything else in your life, you always have time for God. God doesn't want to be second or third. God wants to be number one. Don't neglect your quiet time with God. Don't neglect your Bible study or small groups. Don't neglect your weekly church visits. God has all the time in the world for you so make some time for Him. No matter if you're in a single season or any other season in your life, God should be your number one above anything else.

God, I ask for your forgiveness for those times I've not prioritized my time with you. Forgive me for those times when I placed all those other things above you. I know you are my number one and my everything. Help me to refocus my time and attention on you. In Jesus name I pray. Amen.

Day 33

DON'T STOP PRAYING

Pray without ceasing.

1 Thessalonians 5:17 NASB

This verse is short, simple and to the point. Pray without ceasing. Don't stop praying. No matter what your dating situation looks like, don't stop praying. You may be disheartened by your outlook of ever being married. With every year that passes you don't feel like God is bringing you any closer to marriage. It's been several months or years since you last had a boyfriend. You don't understand why your prayers are going unanswered. You don't understand why you've done the work on you but yet you still don't have a husband nor even a boyfriend. Even if you feel this way don't stop praying.

God wants you to turn to Him regardless of what you see in front of you. He wants you to turn to Him when you feel like there is nothing else you can do. You have a great support system of family and friends but it's only so much they can do for you. God can give you a type of support no one else can give you. Don't get frustrated and stop praying. Keep praying to God for the desires of your heart. Even when you don't think He is, He is working. Keep praying and don't stop. Pray until you feel like you can't pray any longer. God is with you and will bring you marriage and every other thing He has for you. No matter what, don't stop praying.

Lord, I ask that you help me be obedient to your word. Help me to pray without ceasing. Even when I don't think you're answering my prayers, let me continue to turn to you in prayer. I put all my faith in you. Amen.

Day 34

GOD WANTS YOU TO BE WHOLE FIRST

Charm is deceptive and beauty is fleeting, but a

woman who fears the Lord will be praised.

Proverbs 31:30 HCSB

Have you ever tried to bake a cake but only used two of the ten ingredients from the recipe? If you did try to use only those two ingredients, the cake wouldn't turn out right. You probably would end up throwing it away. You would need to use the whole list of ingredients for the cake to have the desired taste of the recipe. Similarly, God doesn't want you to give your husband only a part of yourself to him. He wants you to give your whole self to him. To do this you have to be whole before you ever meet your husband.

You deserve the type of love God has designed for you. You need to be a whole person to receive this type of love. Otherwise, you may not recognize or be able to receive the love when it is presented to you in the form of your husband. God is the only one who can make you whole. You can try to do it on your own but that will get you only so far. You can work on your personality, your looks, your skills, your career, but to truly be whole you will need to have a relationship with God. A woman who fears the Lord will be praised. Not a woman who sometimes fears the Lord or probably fears the Lord, no, a woman who fears the

Lord will be praised. God loves you enough to want you to be whole before you ever meet your husband. Allow God to search your heart and make you whole.

Lord, I ask that you make me whole before I ever meet my husband. I don't know how to become whole without you. Help me to develop a stronger relationship with you. Develop me into the woman you want me to be. In Jesus name. Amen.

Day 35

CONTROL YOUR TONGUE

The words of the reckless pierce like swords, but the

tongue of the wise brings healing.

Proverbs 12:18 NIV

A gentle answer turns away anger, but a harsh word stirs up wrath.

Proverbs 15:1 HCSB

I'm sure you have experienced a time when someone has angered you, mistreated you or hurt you. You were tempted to give them a piece of your mind. You wanted to tell them exactly how they made you feel and what you planned to do about it. Our words have an enormous amount of power. It's important to be very careful how you use those words. Once the words come out of your mouth there is no turning back. You can't simply pick them up and place them back in your mouth. It's key to learn how to control your tongue now before you ever get married.

As a wife, there'll be many times in which you want to let your husband know exactly what's on your mind. There is nothing wrong with open and honest communication but it's all about how you deliver your message. Don't use reckless words just because you're angry, hurt, or even disappointed. These types of words will never help. Remember a gentle answer turns away anger. Practice controlling your tongue right now. Learn how to speak gentle and wise answers and not reckless or harsh ones. Don't wait until you meet your husband to then decide to learn to control your tongue. Start practicing today with your daily interactions with friends, family and co-workers. Gain control over your tongue so one day you can use it to help lift your husband up and not tear him down.

Lord, you know that I struggle in the area of controlling my tongue. I don't always get it right when I try to control it. I can't do it on my own. I need your help. Help me to control my tongue. Let me use my tongue to uplift my husband and others up and not tear them down. Thank you for your grace and mercy when I don't always get it right. Amen.

Day 36

BE READY TO COMPROMISE

Better to live in a wilderness than with a nagging and hot-tempered wife.

Proverbs 21:19 HCSB

B eing a single woman is hard, but it does have its perks. Normally you can have what you want and when you want it, because you are the only one who decides if it's a yes or no. You don't have to consult another person before making a decision. You are the judge and jury in your household. This freedom of choice is great to have. However, you won't always be the one and only judge and jury in your household. There will come a time where you aren't the only person making the decisions. When God brings you into marriage, your actions will now affect your husband as well.

It's time to learn the skills and tools needed now so you won't be resentful when you have to consult your husband before making decisions. Face it, you have become accustomed to not consulting anyone before making a decision. Be prepared to be patient with yourself as there may be an adjustment period. You don't want to use the excuse of you being used to being single to nag your husband into making the decision you want. You don't want to be angry when you don't get your way. This single season is a great time to learn the art of compromise. Ask God for guidance and direction to teach you how to compromise. It may not be easy, but it will be worth it. You want your marriage to be filled with joy and happiness not strife and displeasure. Learn the art of compromise.

> *Father, I ask for your help to learn how to compromise. I'm used to getting my way, Lord, but I know I will need to be able to compromise with the husband you have for me. Give me the knowledge and tools to learn how to do this. In Jesus name. Amen.*

Day 37

BECOME AN EXCELLENT WIFE

An excellent wife, who can find? For her worth is far above jewels.

Proverbs 31:10 NASB

During this single season, you've had time to spend many, many hours thinking about becoming a wife. You probably experienced being excited then maybe nervous when thinking about what it will be like once God brings you marriage. You've read books about how to be a good wife. You have watched videos and talked to many women about preparing to become a wife. You've used the resources provided to you to prepare for marriage and to understand what it means to be a wife. All of this preparation is wonderful and shows you're using your single time wisely. With anything you do you want to do it to your very best ability. Don't become just a good wife, become an excellent wife. God is the one who will show you how to be an excellent wife.

God wants you to be everything He has designed you to be. God wants you to be the excellent wife He has made you to be. No amount of books, videos or conversations can replace the guidance and wisdom God can provide to you. Take your request and desires to God. Take time to be still and listen for His guidance in this area of your life. If you were in control, you would've chosen to be married by now. You would not be in this season of singleness. Yet you are in this single season because God is in control. This is

God's plan for you right now. Use this time to seek wisdom and knowledge from God on how to become the excellent wife He has designed you to be.

Father, thank you that you are the one in control. Thank you that you are giving me time to become everything you have designed me to be as a woman and as a wife. I ask that you give me guidance, knowledge, and wisdom to become the excellent wife you have created me to be. As you are preparing my husband for me, I ask that you prepare me for my husband. Amen.

Day 38

RECOGNIZE WHERE YOU WENT WRONG IN THE PAST

Young lions lack food and go hungry, but those who
seek the Lord will not lack any good thing.
Psalm 34:10 HCSB

You're a daughter of the Most High God. He loves you even when you don't love yourself. He forgives you even when you aren't able to forgive yourself. He knows all the mistakes you made in your past. He doesn't hold those against you. As long as you seek God, you will not lack any good thing. God knows your desire for marriage and won't withhold it from you. He will bring you into marriage with the husband He has picked out for you. However, God wants you to seek Him so that He can bring you marriage and all the other good things He has in store for you. Recognize that the way you've been going about marriage is all wrong. Acknowledge where you went wrong in the past.

In the past, you can admit you gave God your checklist for what you wanted in a husband. Then you met a guy you really liked and started praying about him. Instead of praying for God to let you know whether he was the man He had for you, you prayed that God would change him into the man He had for you. Although you sought God, you tried to control the situation. This time around stop trying to control things. Stop trying to make it happen.

Recognize where you went wrong with this approach in your past. Know who really is in control. Seek God during your single season. Surrender control to Him. As long as you seek God and His will for your life, He will not withhold any good thing from you including marriage.

Father, thank you for your forgiveness. Thank you for your grace. Thank you for helping me to recognize where I went wrong in my past. I ask that you help me to surrender all control to you. I know I can't make things happen on my own. I seek you Lord. Amen.

Day 39

BE COMPLETELY HEALED FROM YOUR PAST

He heals the brokenhearted and binds up their wounds.

Psalm 147:3 NASB

Take a minute and think about how many people have come and gone in your life. How many friends have you let go of along the way? How many men have you dated or been intimate with when you knew you shouldn't? How many times have you been disappointed by family and friends? How many times have you tried to no avail? Take time to reflect over all those situations and people in your life that didn't turn out the way you thought they would. There is no need to feel sad or regret any of those people or situations. These things are your past. It's okay to have a past because everyone has one. Your past hurts made you into the woman you are today. It's important to remember your past so that you can be completely healed from it.

God doesn't want to bring you your husband while you are still a wounded woman. He doesn't want you to take your hurts and pains out on your husband. He doesn't want you to be so hurt from your past that it prevents you from loving the man He has for you. God knows you have experienced heartbreak and pain. He knows you've been hurt deeply by family, friends, and maybe even men. God knows your pain and wants you to allow Him to heal you. He will patch up those wounds if you let Him. A part of healing from your past is forgiving those who have wronged you. Don't continue to live with bitterness and hurt. Let God work on you. Allow God to heal you of your past.

> *God, I come to you today asking that you heal me of my past. You know who has hurt me and you know how they hurt me. Help me to forgive them and to forgive myself. Help me to let go so I can be set free. Heal my heart Father. Amen.*

Day 40

YOU ALREADY HAVE
THE INSTRUCTIONS

If you ask Me anything in My name, I will do it.

John 14:14 NASB

Sometimes we like to make things more complicated than they have to be. God's word already gives us instructions on things that we want. The word says to ask God anything in His name and He will do it. Simply put if you have a desire for marriage that is in God's will, ask Him for it. You don't have to figure out how you will get married. God's word already gives you the instructions to just ask Him for marriage. However, asking is the easy part.

Once you ask God for marriage, believe that what you've asked will come to pass. Trust God at His word. Believe that His promises are Yes and Amen. There is no need to ask God for marriage if you won't display the faith to believe God will bring you what you have asked for. Don't continue to try to control when and how you get married. Once you ask God for marriage, let it go. Focus your time on deepening your relationship with God. Focus your time on becoming the woman and the wife God has made you to be. Have faith and trust God hears you when you ask in His name. God will do just what He said He will do. He has never let you down before and He won't start now.

Father, thank you for giving me the instructions to ask for what I want. Thank you that the things in your will are already done. Help me to keep my faith in you. Help me to always remember that your promises are Yes and Amen. In Jesus name I pray. Amen.

Day 41

ACCEPT THE MAN GOD HAS FOR YOU TO MARRY

It's better to have a partner than go it alone. Share the work, share the wealth. And if one falls down, the other helps. But if there's no one to help, tough! Two in a bed warm each other. Alone, you shiver all night. By yourself you're unprotected. With a friend you can face the worst. Can you round up a third? A three-stranded rope isn't easily snapped.

Ecclesiastes 4:9-12 MSG

God's word tells us it's better to have a partner than go it alone. This word should encourage you. God himself is acknowledging that He wants you to have a partner to do life with. All through these verses are reasons why having a partner is better than not having a partner. As you read these verses recognize that God wants you to be married and have a partner to do life with. There are very few people that God has called to singleness. There is a good chance that if you have a desire for marriage God probably hasn't called you to singleness.

God wants you to be married just as much as you want to be. The Lord has designed you to have a partner in your husband. He wants you and your husband to be connected with Him and form a three-stranded rope. Right now, all you can do is keep seeking God. Pray that your future husband is also seeking God. With the two of you seeking God separately, you will come together and have God in your marriage and in your life. When God brings you your husband, accept him for who he is. You can ask God to bring you your husband but not be happy with the person He brings. Yes, pray specific prayers regarding the traits and attributes that you desire in your husband. However, don't be too rigid and miss out on the husband God has for you because he is missing a few items. During your singleness continue to pray and ask God for guidance so that you will recognize your husband when He sends him to you. Be ready and willing to accept the man God has for you.

Lord Jesus, help me to accept the man you bring into my life as my husband. Let me not be blinded by him not having everything I want. Don't let me overlook him. God give me clarity and guidance to know who my husband is. Father let me accept the man you have for me to marry. In Jesus name I pray. Amen.

Day 42

SURROUND YOURSELF WITH WISE WOMEN

Now if any of you lacks wisdom, he should ask God, who gives
to all generously and without criticizing, and it will be given to
him. But let him ask in faith without doubting. For the doubter
is like the surging sea, driven and tossed by the wind.

James 1:5-6 HCSB

This season of singleness is a great time to gain more wisdom. Don't just pray for God to bring you marriage, pray for God to give you wisdom. Seek God to gain the wisdom you will need to be a wife. Being a wife will not be an easy task; you will need wisdom to know what decisions to make. You will need wisdom to know how to forgive and love your husband no matter what. You will need a wisdom that only God can send your way. Ask God to not only give you wisdom but to surround you with wise women in your life.

Wise women can serve as powerful tools on your journey to marriage. Seek out not only wise women but wise wives. Spend time picking their brains for advice. Take time to have conversations with them to learn about their marriages. Find out what mistakes and mishaps they have made along the way. You don't have to make the same mistakes if you can learn how to avoid them. Wise women can help you to become wise beyond your age. No matter how old you are, there is always a wise woman from whom you can learn from. Ask God for wisdom and He will give you wisdom. He will give you wisdom and send wise people to surround you. Be open and ready to learn from the wise women God puts in your life.

Father, your word tells me to ask for wisdom and you will give it to me. I ask that you give me wisdom far beyond my years. Surround me with wise women in my life. Help me to learn from them and grow to become the wife and the woman you have made me to be. Amen.

Day 43

GOD IS PREPARING YOU FOR MARRIAGE

Wives, submit yourselves to your husbands, as is fitting in the Lord.

Husbands, love your wives and do not be harsh with them.

Colossians 3:18-19 NIV

Submission this and submission that. A wife is supposed to submit to her husband. That's what you're taught if you step foot in any church. You may have seen it modeled by your mom or another woman in your life. This verse is always brought up in a sermon or Bible study about single women becoming wives. Yes, you know you are supposed to submit to your husband, but do you know exactly what that means? Being submissive to your husband gets misconstrued and sometimes has a negative connotation. Many well-meaning individuals in your life have tried to teach you what submission means, or maybe no one has tried to teach you what submission means. It's time to stop looking at everyone else to teach you what it means to be submissive to your husband and ask God to lead and guide you to show you what it means to be submissive to your husband.

While you are single, God is preparing you for marriage. God is developing you into a submissive wife. As long as you seek God, He will continue to show you how to be a submissive wife. This is the Lord's design for wives.

In this season, be vigilant and see all the ways God is preparing you to be a submissive wife. Be open and ready to do what He wants you to do in this season so that He can continue to prepare you for marriage. God loves you and wants you to be the wife He has designed you to be. Don't be discouraged because you're still single. God has given you extra time to prepare for marriage. God is a good and faithful God. He knows exactly what He is doing. Take the time He is giving you and prepare for your marriage.

Father, I want to know what it means to be a submissive wife. I want to know how to be the wife and the woman you have designed me to be. Help me to be open and willing to go and do what you want me to do in this season. Help me to believe in your process as you prepare me for marriage. Amen.

Day 44

HAVE YOU MADE MARRIAGE AN IDOL

Oh, let me warn you, sisters in Jerusalem: Don't excite love,

don't stir it up, until the time is ripe – and you're ready.

Song of Songs 8:4 MSG

Have you ever met a man that you were just head over hills for? Have you ever met a man who you just knew was "The One"? When you're in love, it is an amazing feeling. We become extremely excited and are so glad to have someone. Being in love is terrific when you're in love with the man God has for you. If he isn't the right man for you, it can be extremely painful and far too problematic. It's important to love the man God has for you instead of loving just any man that says he loves you.

God knows when the time is right to send you love. He will send you a love that you will know is designed by Him. Don't hurry into things with a man just because you're in love or what you think is love. Listen to the Holy Spirit's leading more than you listen to your feelings. Consult God while you are falling in love. Make sure that he is the man God has for you. There is nothing worse than falling in love with a man that's not sent to you by God. Don't become so discouraged and eager to marry that marriage becomes an idol. Don't desire marriage more than you desire God. Don't want a man more than you want the man

God has for you. God is preparing you for marriage with the husband He has picked out for you. Don't rush and try to speed things along. God will awaken your love when the time is right.

> *Lord, search my heart and show me the ways I have made marriage an idol. I desire you more than I desire marriage. I want to love you before I ever love a man. Help me to not excite love before it is time. Bring love to me when you see fit. Amen.*

Day 45

EVERYONE IS GETTING MARRIED BUT ME

Keep asking, and it will be given to you. Keep searching, and you will find. Keep knocking, and the door will be opened to you. For everyone who asks receives, and the one who searches finds, and to the one who knocks, the door will be opened.

Matthew 7:7-8 HCSB

The HCSB translation of this verse is wonderful because it says to keep asking, keep searching and keep knocking. This sums up what single women should do. We all know being single when you desire marriage is no easy task. You want someone to love and for someone to love you. You want someone to have by your side. You want someone you can trust and let your guard down around. You feel like everyone around you is getting married but you. You don't understand why you're still single when you try your best to be obedient to God. You feel like you're doing everything God has asked of you but yet you are still single. Even when you don't think God hears you, keep going. Even when you don't see anything changing, keep going.

God hears your prayers. He sees your obedience. He knows you cry some days. He knows some days you can't even cry because you are so weary. He knows you desire marriage. You have to trust God in this difficult season of prolonged waiting. Keep asking, keep searching, keep knocking. Your efforts are not in vain. God's word tells you it will be given to you, you will find, and the door will be opened to you. If you ask you will receive it, if you search you will find it, and if you knock the door will be opened to you. It doesn't say you may receive it, you may find it or the door may be opened to you. It says will. God will bring you marriage according to His will. God will bring you marriage in His perfect timing. Until then keep asking, searching and knocking. God will answer.

Father, I am getting discouraged. It feels like everyone is getting married but me. At times I feel like I'm losing hope. Help me Lord to keep asking. Help me to keep searching and help me to keep knocking. Lord strengthen my faith and trust in you. Amen.

Day 46

WAIT ON HIM

Wait for the Lord; Be strong and let your heart take courage;

Yes, wait for the Lord.

Psalm 27:14 NASB

God has extraordinary plans in store for you. He designed his plans perfectly to give you everything you will ever need. The mistakes you will make along the way are already factored into His plans. God's plans already account for those days when you will feel frustrated and discouraged. God knew at this exact moment you would be in this waiting season. God knew all of this because His plans are always better than our plans. He knows everything that you'll face because it's all according to His plan.

God's plan has you single now but one day you won't be single. One day God will bring you that husband He has for you. You have to wait on God to bring him to you though. Be strong and keep waiting on God. He is the only one that can give you your heart's desires. Yet waiting is easier said than done. When you're tired of waiting just keep waiting a little more. God will give you the strength to keep waiting. Don't try to move before it's time. Don't try to rush to make things happen. Place your trust in God and keep anticipating all that He will do. Be still and wait on Him because your singleness is all according to His plan.

God, thank you that your plans are so much better than my plans. Give me the strength to wait on you even when I'm frustrated. Help me to be patient when I want to follow my own plans instead of your plans. Thank you for your grace when I try to do things my way. Father help me to be still and wait on you. Amen.

Day 47

LEARN HOW TO LOVE
BEFORE MARRIAGE

Love is patient, love is kind. It does not envy, it does not boast,
it is not proud. It does not dishonor others, it is not self-
seeking, it is not easily angered, it keeps no record of wrongs.
Love does not delight in evil but rejoices with the truth. It always
protects, always trusts, always hopes, always perseveres.
1 Corinthians 13:4-7 NIV

The Bible gives us the blueprint on love. This very familiar passage describes to us how God intends for us to love. It highlights just how important love really is. You can have so many other things but if you don't have love it won't be the same. God knows that you're still single, but He does want you to have love. He knows how much you desire to be married and to love and be loved. Your Heavenly Father is going to take care of you and bring you love when the time is right.

While waiting on God to bring you into marriage learn how to really love. Learn to have a love like this passage says. Study this passage to discover the way you should love your husband. Marriage is not the time to learn how to love. That is not the time to try to figure out exactly what love means. Yes, marriage will help you learn to love even more but you can spend this time now learning how to love before you ever get married. Learn what it means to be patient, kind and forgiving towards others. You don't need a husband to practice those things. Learn to love those around you and those you encounter daily. Learn how to be selfless and take others' needs into consideration. Let this time before marriage be used to strengthen your skills in love. God gives us the blueprint on how to love. Now it's time to start practicing love before you ever get married.

Father, thank you for showing me how to love through your love for me. Thank you for putting in your word the ways to love. Help me as I want to learn to love the way you have designed love to be. I can't do this without you Lord. I ask for you to help me on my journey. Amen.

Day 48

IT'S OKAY TO BE AFRAID

When I am afraid, I will trust You.

Psalm 56:3 HCSB

At this present moment there is only one word to describe how you feel, afraid. You're afraid that you'll continue to spend holidays and birthdays as a single woman. You're afraid that you'll continue to celebrate those big moments as a single woman. You're afraid that time will continue to pass you by. You're afraid that happily ever after may never come. You're afraid that your prayers won't be heard and that your cries will go unseen. It's okay to be afraid. Being afraid is a normal human emotion. You don't have to pretend. The fact is you continue to remain single month after month and year after year. You're afraid that God won't ever bring you into marriage. You're afraid He doesn't hear you. It's okay.

You're not alone in how you feel. Many people fail to admit it, but at some point, we all feel afraid. It's okay to feel afraid at times but when you do feel afraid turn to God. Don't let your fears stop you from believing. Seek God when you feel afraid. Have confidence in Him to calm your fears. Don't worry anymore about being single. Don't be afraid any longer. Continue to have faith no matter how you feel. When you are afraid, trust Him.

Lord, I don't want to admit it but I'm afraid. I'm afraid that you won't give me the desires of my heart. Forgive me for my fear and my unbelief. Allow me to trust you even when I am afraid. Give me the courage to trust you. In Jesus name. Amen.

Day 49

I'M DOING EVERYTHING RIGHT BUT NOTHING IS HAPPENING

Yet those who wait for the Lord will gain new strength; They will mount up with wings like eagles. They will run and not get tired. They will walk and not become weary.

Isaiah 40:31 NASB

You have spent many days fasting and praying. You've changed into a better woman. You've deepened your relationship with God. You've changed who you hang around and the places you go. Quite frankly, you have cleaned up your act and know you're ready to be a wife. It's easy to get upset when you feel like you're doing everything right, but nothing is happening. You continue to be single no matter what you do. You just don't understand why you are still single. You may even start questioning God and become angry because you are still single even though you feel like you are doing everything right.

Sometimes we aren't able to explain the why of things. Even if we're doing everything right, occasionally God chooses to let us remain in a season of singleness. During this prolonged season you are probably weary and tired. You may be ready to give up on doing it God's way. You may be ready to give up on being married or ever being in love. It's hard but just keep waiting. Don't give up on God because He never has and never will give up on you. Wait on the Lord. When you wait on the Lord, He will give you a strength to wait that you didn't know you possessed. Continue to push doing this waiting season. Don't grow tired. Don't become weary. Keep trusting God because this waiting season won't last forever.

Father, at times I feel weary. Give me strength Lord because I am growing tired of this waiting season. Help me Lord to wait on you. Give me a power to wait that I don't know I have. Lord help me to keep walking and keep running toward you. Amen.

Day 50

HE WILL DO WHAT HE SAID HE WILL DO

Blessed is she who has believed that the Lord would fulfill

his promises to her!

Luke 1:45 NIV

A re you praying for certain things and situations, but you aren't sure if God will actually bring you those things or change those situations? Are you praying for marriage and hoping God will answer your prayers? Are you praying for God to bring you your husband but in the back of your mind you aren't 100% sure He will? If you answered yes to any of these questions, it's time to change your mindset. Have faith that God will do what He said He will do. Believe that your prayers are being answered. Trust that God is listening to every single one of your prayers.

God is never late. God never loses a battle. God's promises are Yes and Amen. God will do what His word says He will do. You don't have to doubt or second guess. God's word tells you that He will give you the desires of your heart that are according to His will. Spend time praying to know God's will for your life. Don't spend your time frustrated, angry and doubting God. Pray those prayers to God and believe that what the Lord has said will be accomplished. Study your word and get to know what God has promised you. Be in a position to recognize when God is doing just what He said He will do. He will never fail you. He is the only one you can always trust to keep every single promise. He will do what He said He will do. Place your faith in Him.

Lord, thank you that your promises are Yes and Amen. Thank you for doing just what you said you will do. Help me to know your will for my life. Give me the faith to keep trusting you regardless of what my circumstances look like. Restore my faith and help my unbelief. In Jesus name I pray. Amen.

Day 51

HE WILL ALWAYS ANSWER

Call to me and I will answer you. I'll tell you marvelous and
wondrous things that you could never figure out on your own.

Jeremiah 33:3 MSG

Have you ever had a topic you really wanted to discuss with someone but when you called them, they didn't answer? Have you ever had a question that you needed answered but when you called on someone to answer it, they didn't answer? There will be many times in your life when you will call out to people for support, encouragement, and help but they won't answer. People don't intentionally let you down but they will let you down from time to time. God is the one person who will never let you down. No matter the day or the hour when you call, He will always answer.

Call on God when you're at your breaking point. You don't want to spend the rest of your life single, but you don't know what else to do. Call on God when you need to know what His next step is for your life. Call on God to give you the guidance to know who your husband is. God wants you to call on Him when you're ready to try to take control and date that guy He told you not to date. Call Him when you're ready to read that book or watch that movie you know will only tempt you. God is there to answer you whenever you call Him. God is there to answer you even if you don't have the strength to call on Him. God will always answer you no matter the situation and no matter the time. He loves you and will always take care of you.

God, I love you and need you. Thank you for always being there to answer when I call on you. Help me to call on you in the good and in the bad. Give me the courage and the faith to call on you no matter the situation. Thank you for your love. Amen.

Day 52

HE'S ALREADY PLANNED IT

*I know what I'm doing. I have it all planned out, plans to take
care of you, not abandon you, plans to give you the future you
hope for. When you call on me, when you come and pray to me,
I'll listen. When you come looking for me, you'll find me.*

Jeremiah 29:11-13 MSG

God knew that you would still be in a season of
singleness right now. God knew that you would be
reading this devotional looking for a little encouragement. God already knows everything that will happen
in your life. He's already planned it out. Before you were
born God already had the plans for your life mapped out.
God understands that you desire marriage and already has
the plan for how He will bring you your husband. God's
plans will take care of you and give you your heart's desires. You don't have to worry about what's coming up
next.

God has great plans for you that you can't even imagine right now. His plans are far greater than anything you
would have even planned for yourself. He doesn't want you
to rely on the things you've planned for your life. He wants
you to call on Him because He is listening. He wants you
to come looking for Him. God doesn't want you looking
to anyone else or anywhere else. Pursue God to know His
plans. Seek to understand His will for your life. Let God's
will be done in your life and not your own will. Be obedi-

ent to the plan God has for you . No matter how long it takes, stick to God's plan so He will bring you into the marriage He has for you. Trust Him.

Lord, I know that you already have marriage planned out for me. Forgive me for trying to plan it out on my own. Help me to trust in your will and plans for my life. I don't want to keep doing the things I want to do. I want your will to be done in my life. Amen.

Day 53

ASK HIM, THEN BELIEVE HIM

This is the confidence we have in approaching God: that if we ask anything

according to his will, he hears us. And if we know that he hears us—

whatever we ask—we know that we have what we asked of him.

1 John 5:14-15 NIV

God's word tells you to ask anything according to His will. It is discouraging when you keep praying and praying but nothing seems to be happening. You keep asking God for marriage but then you continue to remain single. You've been single for so many years that it feels like marriage is never going to happen. It feels like your prayers have fallen on deaf ears. It feels like you're only wasting your breath. Don't feel this way because God's word says that He hears you.

Believe that God hears your prayers. Know that whatever you ask you will have if it is according to His will. Those prayers of you crying out to God for something to change are heard. Those prayers are not in vain. God hears you even when you think He doesn't. Even when the noise of life is too loud and you don't have all the words to pray, God still hears you. Trust and believe Him at His word. When you ask God for marriage have the confidence to believe that He will bring you marriage. This single season is lasting longer than you expected, but it won't last forever. Keep praying to God and asking Him for what it is you desire. God will hear you and give you what you ask for according to His will.

> *Father, help me to believe that what I ask you for you will give me. Restore my confidence in believing in who you are and what your word says. Give me courage to keep asking and then to believe you even if I can't see how or when. Let my prayers be filled with confidence in you Father. Amen.*

Day 54

YOU ARE ENOUGH

Then the Lord God said, "It is not good for the man to be
alone; I will make him a helper suitable for him."

Genesis 2:18 NASB

There is a great deal of pressure all around us to conform to what we see on TV and on social media. You can be led to believe that if you don't match a certain set of criteria then there is something wrong with you. It's tempting to want to change your looks, your personality, and other aspects of who you are. It feels like who you are is not enough. It feels like you need more of this or more of that, then God will send you your husband. The truth is right here in this exact moment "You Are Enough".

God has made you just the way He intended for you to be. You're perfect just the way you are. As His word says, God has made you a helper for the husband He has for you. He's made you a suitable mate for your husband. You don't have to change anything about yourself. God has not only made you enough for your husband, but He has made you enough period. If God decides to never bring you marriage, you are still enough. Don't try to be more like the people on your left and on your right. Be more like that person you see in the mirror. Look in the mirror and know that woman staring back at you is enough. God will bring you your husband in His perfect timing. You won't have to change to fit who you think He wants you to be. God will bring you a husband who looks at you and says you are not only enough, but you are more than enough.

God, sometimes I feel discouraged and think that I am not enough. Sometimes Lord I think that I am still single because I'm not good enough. I ask that you remove those negative thoughts from my mind. Give me the confidence to know that I am enough. Help me to trust you and know that you have designed me just the way you wanted me to be. Give me the courage to be who you have created me to be. Amen.

Day 55

STAY WATCHFUL

Don't allow love to turn into lust, setting off a downhill slide

into sexual promiscuity, filthy practices, or bullying greed.

Ephesians 5:3 MSG

Have you met someone you think could be your husband? Do you feel like God may be revealing to you who your husband is? This is a great feeling to be that much closer to marriage. Although you may finally see the light at the end of the tunnel, you have to stay watchful to avoid temptation. Don't let your guard down. Don't become so excited or fall so deeply in love that you lose sight of what God's word says. You've done a great job of following God's direction for dating and now you have to work even harder to follow His direction.

After spending years single, it's a feeling of pure excitement and joy to finally have met the husband God has for you. The two of you have to stay strong and remember all the work you've put in up until now. Stay in the word and continue to fight temptation. Even if you fell to temptation in the past, now is the time to keep those lustful thoughts and behaviors at bay. Ask for God to give you the strength to not fall into temptation. Don't try to take control of things and rush into marriage. Continue to seek God and let him lead your dating and your relationship. Stay watchful and let God keep the control.

Father, I know that I am so close to marriage right now. The temptation is getting harder and harder to fight. I ask for you to give me the strength to fight temptation. Don't let me fall to lust. I ask for your help to continue. Amen.

Day 56

THERE SEEMS TO BE
NO LIGHT AT THE END
OF THE TUNNEL

The Lord is good to those who wait for Him, to the person who seeks

Him. It is good to wait quietly for deliverance from the Lord.

Lamentations 3:25-26 HCSB

I know you are exhausted. I know you are worn out. I
know you are discouraged. You keep reading all the
scriptures about waiting on God. People keep telling
you to keep trusting in God. You know the word says to
put all your faith and trust in Him. It's clear that at the end
of the day all you can really do is keep seeking God. Even
though you know what you need to do, it doesn't make it
any easier.

There seems to be no light at the end of the tunnel.
All you can see at the end of this tunnel of singleness is
darkness. You keep trying to stay positive, keep praying
and keep seeking God but it doesn't seem to make a light
appear at the end of that tunnel. It feels like it's always
going to be dark. It feels like you will always walk through
a tunnel of darkness with no light in sight. I know you feel
like this single season will never end but it will. People
keep telling you this is just a season, and this too shall pass.
You hear them but it's still hard to believe it won't always
be darkness at the end of the tunnel. Don't stop believ-

ing. There will be a light. Just keep looking to the Lord no matter how difficult that becomes. God is your light even when you can't see the light. He will deliver you from this single season in His perfect timing. Don't be discouraged. God's light shines bright enough to keep you going through the darkest tunnel. He is walking with you every step of the way. He won't leave you. Keep seeking and trusting God no matter what. One day you will see the light at the end of the tunnel.

Father, hear my prayers. I am exhausted and I feel discouraged. I don't see a light at the end of this tunnel of singleness. I don't see when you will ever bring me out of this single season. Father help me stay encouraged. I cry out to you. Give me the strength to wait for you Lord. Amen.

Day 57

MAYBE GOD'S WORKING ON YOU

Let's take a good look at the way we're living and reorder

our lives under God. Let's lift our hearts and hands at one

and the same time, praying to God in heaven.

Lamentations 3:40-41 MSG

On occasions, we can become so busy with life. We have so many obligations both professionally and personally. You're single but still want to enjoy yourself. You have a good healthy social life filled with many friends and family. You're faithful with your church attendance. You may even have a couple of small groups you attend. You're single but you keep yourself busy. That is great; however, as the verse says take a good look at the way you are living. Maybe it's time to reorder your life around God.

Busyness may feel like the only way to make it through this season of singleness, but it's not always the answer. It's time you evaluate the amount of time all your activities have taken away from God. Maybe you have been so active that you've been too busy to even spend quality time with God. Your Father wants you to get to know Him on an even deeper level. He wants you to know how much He loves you and will take care of you. Take a moment to stop long enough to spend time with God. God could be using your time single to work on you. You've been living your life the way God wants you to.... mostly. But God wants you to live your life according to His will 100% of the time. Consider that God may want to do more work on you before He brings you into marriage. Spend more of your time with God. Let this time be more intimate. Truly seek to grow closer and deepen your relationship with the Lord. Let Him work on you and move in your life during this time.

Lord, forgive me for trying to fill my life with busyness instead of filling my life with you. Give me the guidance and wisdom to know the balance between healthy busyness and unhealthy busyness. In all that I do help me to keep you as my first priority. Help me to seek you above everything else. In Jesus name. Amen.

Day 58

GIVE ALL YOUR WORRIES TO GOD

Cast all your anxiety on him because he cares for you.

1 Peter 5:7 NIV

I know you are anxious. You don't want to constantly think about if you'll ever get married but it's hard not to. With every day that passes you're getting a little older. Perhaps an important milestone birthday is approaching, and you always wanted to be married by the time you hit that birthday. You've been single for so long that you wonder if you will remember how to even be in a relationship with a man. Maybe you've never had a boyfriend and you are worried you won't know how to be in a romantic relationship. You have so many worries about the future. Even though you are worried, God doesn't want His daughter to worry. He wants you to give all your worries to Him. Let Him handle the worrying.

God loves you and God cares for you. He doesn't want you to spend this single season worried, frustrated, and weary. He wants you to enjoy this season. He wants you to travel, learn new things and pick up new hobbies. Take the energy you spend worrying and place it toward developing a more intimate connection with Him. Don't stress yourself out worrying about the details of your husband and your marriage. God knows what His plans are for you. Cast all your anxiety, worries, and fears on the Lord. He will help to ease them all. Don't fret over what you can't see, trust God is working it all out just for you.

Father, help me to stop worrying about who my husband is and when I will get married. I give you my fears, my worries, and my anxiety. Help my faith to be strong. Allow me to continue to believe and trust in your perfect design for my life. Amen.

Day 59

DON'T GIVE UP

But me, I'm not giving up. I'm sticking around to see what God will do. I'm waiting for God to make things right. I'm counting on God to listen to me.

Micah 7:7 MSG

Many more months may pass by. Many more years may pass by. It may not be time for God to bring you the husband He has for you. The road for trusting and waiting on God's timing is tough. It's hard. It's scary. It's lonely. No matter how long the road is, don't give up. No matter how isolated, anxious or sad you feel don't give up. Even if you feel like you're all alone, you're not because God is walking with you. If it is God's will for your life, you will be married.

Continue to wait on God to make things right. Keep trusting in Him and what He will do. Don't give up on your prayers and your obedience to God. Trust that God is listening to you no matter how faint your cry or how small the whisper. God hears you loud and clear. When you're at the end, don't give up. Just when you think you can't go on God will be right there to hold your hand. When you're in your deepest valley, He will give you His hand to lift you out. Living as a single Christian woman is difficult, but it is possible. Don't settle for less than God's best for your life. Don't give up on God because He has a Godly husband picked out just for you.

Lord, I know that your word is clear. I know that you tell me to wait on you. Father I ask that you give me the tenacity and humility to wait on you. Don't let me give up on you. I know you love me and have my best interest at heart. Thank you for always listening to my prayers. Thank you for always hearing my cries. Thank you, Father, for the husband you have for me. In Jesus name. Amen.

Day 60

WHAT IF YOU NEVER
GET MARRIED

And don't be wishing you were someplace else or with someone

else. Where you are right now is God's place for you. Live and obey

and love and believe right there. God, not your marital status,

defines your life. Don't think I'm being harder on you than on

the others. I give this same counsel in all the churches.

1 Corinthians 7:17 MSG

This season of singleness is exactly where God wants you to be. Don't continue to look around and wish you were married like others. Don't look at the pictures on social media and wish you had the life someone else has. God has you precisely where He wants you to be right now. Come to a place where you can accept this season of singleness God has you in currently. Don't concern yourself with when it will change. Don't worry yourself about if it is going to change. God's word tells you God, not your marital status, defines your life.

Although you desire marriage, if it's not God's will for you, you may never get married. This is a tough pill to swallow. Ask yourself: do you desire God more or do you desire what He can do for you more? Accept that God's will for you is far greater than anything you can ever imagine. If God's will for you is to never get married, you have to be able to accept that. Want God's will for you more than you want your own will. Desire to love God more than you desire what God will do for you. God has not called many people to singleness. However, if you are one of the ones He has called, you will have everything you need. God will give you all the strength, encouragement, fulfillment and love you will ever need. Get to a place in your life where you're satisfied even if you never get married. It isn't a punishment. It just means God has other plans for you. He doesn't make mistakes. Whatever He has called you to, it is according to His perfect plan. Accept God and His plan for you no matter what it is.

Lord, bring me to a place where I desire your will more than I desire my own will. Even if your will is not what I imagined for my life, help me to follow your will for my life. Lord you know my desires. Give me the desires of my heart that are according to your will. Give me the ability to accept whatever you have for me. In Jesus name. Amen.

AFTERWORD

Thank you for taking time to read this devotional. I pray it will continue to help you stay encouraged on your single journey. I wanted to share with you my single journey and the scriptures that help me. I hope that the words of this devotional helped you in some way, no matter how small. We all know at least one single woman in our lives. No matter what you see on the outside, every single woman can use just a little more encouragement. I ask that you leave a review and send a copy to that single woman in your life. If that single woman is you, I pray that these devotions gave you the encouragement you need to keep trusting in God and waiting on Him to bring you your husband.

Contact: taliah.aneesah@gmail.com